M000232981

Pilot 101

How to Become a Pilot and Achieve Success in Your Aviation Career From A to Z

HowExpert with Jeffrey Lawrence

For more tips related to this topic, visit www.HowExpert.com/pilot.

Recommended Resources

www.HowExpert.com – Quick 'How To' Guides on Unique Topics by Everyday Experts.

www.HowExpert.com/writers - Write About Your #1 Passion/Knowledge/Experience.

www.HowExpert.com/membership - Learn a New 'How To' Topic About Practically Everything Every Week.

www.HowExpert.com/jobs - Check Out HowExpert Jobs.

Table of Contents

Introduction

There are many reasons you might want to become a pilot. First, it is something that is not for everyone, yet entirely possible if that is what you want to do. Just being a pilot sets a person apart from the crowd. There are more than 325 million people in the United States, yet there are little more than 600,000 pilots among that population—less than 0.2%.

And if you ever thought about flying as a career—now is the time. There were more than 827,000 pilots in 1987, yet today, the number is a little more than 600,000, and the one industry that needs pilots and is being hit hard by the emerging shortage is the airline industry.

During the 1960s through the 1970s, the U. S. military was training thousands of pilots for the Cold War and Vietnam requirements. The demand for military pilots has dropped significantly, and the supply of military-trained pilots for the airlines has decreased significantly.

There are many ways to enjoy flying and, if that is your goal, make a career of aviation.

Chapter 1. Piloting Options

There are several ways to select what you want to fly. Most pilots start out in small fixed-wing training aircraft, and then move on, if they want to, to what they really want to fly. The four main categories of aircraft as defined by the Federal Aviation Administration (FAA) are: "airplane," "rotorcraft." "glider," and "lighter-than-air." Deciding what you want to fly will determine and direct your training. But, do not be surprised if "what you want to fly" changes along the way!

You have several different categories of aircraft from which to choose.

1. Category: Airplanes

Airplanes are any aircraft with engines and wings. There are single-seat sport airplanes to 300-plus passenger airliners to heavy-lift transport airplanes. This also includes the fighter aircraft of the Air Force and Navy.

a. Airplanes are the choice if travel is part of your plan.
b. Airplanes are the least expensive when it comes to learning to fly.
c. You can build your own airplane and fly it safely.
d. A 4-seat airplane can easily take a family of four 400 miles or more in a morning. Where would you like to go?

e. Airplanes—aerobatic ones—offer about the onl-
   way to see the world from upside down, if that
   is on your list of things to do.

2. Category: Rotorcraft (Helicopters, Gyroplanes)

Not everyone flies airplanes. Rotorcraft are an entirely
different category of aircraft that offers capabilities
that most airplanes cannot achieve, including vertical
takeoff and landing and hovering.

   a. You could keep a small helicopter in the family
      garage and take off from the yard.
   b. Most helicopters are best suited for shorter
      trips.
   c. There are many professional opportunities
      such as in the military, flying medivac and
      emergency rescue helicopters, traffic reporters,
      sightseeing tours, etc.

3. Category: Gliders

A sailplane or glider is an airplane without an engine.
It requires a tow-plane to pull it up into the air to
launch it.

   a. Skilled glider pilots can soar for hours under
      the right conditions.

b. Sailplane flying is essentially a sport, i.e., there is no other reason to fly them than for enjoyment or as an instructor.
c. There is something very special about flying without the sound of a loud engine pulling you through the air.

4. Category: Lighter-Than-Air (Blimps or Hot Air Balloons)

If you want to just "hang out" and watch the scenery drift by—literally—you may want to investigate hot-air ballooning. Or if cruising at a very leisurely pace appeals to you, you could become one of the very few blimp pilots.

a. A hot air balloon is truly quiet, except when the burner is filling the balloon with heated air.
b. There is something magical about several dozen colorful hot air balloons drifting across the sky.
c. This category also includes "airships." These are aircraft such as blimps, and, historically, dirigibles.
d. These are the airships seen flying over major sporting and other events.
e. There continue to be indications that large airships may reappear as specialized transports of the future.

Chapter 2. Personal Flying

There are two broad categories of pilots: private pilots and professional pilots. Private pilots fly for personal reasons and may not be paid for (earn income from) their flying. There are different levels of certificates for both "private" flying and professional flying.

A Word About Logbooks: Every pilot is expected to obtain and maintain a logbook of his or her flying time and the nature of those flights. The logbook is a legal record of all flight training, signed by the instructor pilot, as well all flying that needs to be documented to demonstrate training and recency of experience. For example, to carry passengers after dark, the pilot must have an instructor's endorsement for night flight or show that he has made at least three night takeoffs and landings within the past 90 days.

Certificates and Ratings: A "Certificate" or license is the document issued for specific levels of piloting skill: Private Pilot Certificate, Sport Pilot Certificate, Commercial Pilot Certificate, Airline Transport Pilot Certificate, etc.

A "Rating" is a privilege that is added to a Certificate. For example, a Private Pilot may add an instrument "rating" or "seaplane" rating to his certificate.

1. Student Pilot Certificate

The student pilot certificate is issued by the Aviation Medical Examiner who perform the student's initial exam. The certificate is part of the medical form issued to the student pilot.

2. Private Pilot Certificate

The Private Pilot Certificate (or Private Pilot License (PPL)) is the foundation for all further flight training. But it also provides the pilot with broad privileges including almost unlimited travel.

A pilot certificate must also include a "rating," indicating the general type of aircraft the pilot is permitted to fly. Most pilots start out with a single-engine airplane, land rating. But, with additional training, the Private Pilot can be rated to fly, for example, multi-engine aircraft or seaplanes.

Privileges and Limitations: A Private Pilot's Certificate makes is possible to visit friends or family who live too far for a convenient drive. A typical personal airplane can carry four people at a speed of 120 mph or more in a straight line to your destination, avoiding traffic, stop signs, and stoplights. Most communities have local airports that will be near your destination.

The Private Pilot may carry passengers but may not carry passengers or cargo for hire. Your passengers may share the cost of a flight. For example, you rent a 4-seat aircraft for $80.00 and take three people for a ride for an hour. Each passenger may contribute $20.00—one-fourth or his share—to help pay for the flight.

You may not get paid for flying, but you may fly in the furtherance of business. If you need to visit clients who may be several hundred miles away, you may fly to airports near the client. You may deduct the expenses as you would if you drove your personal vehicle.

The fact is you may enjoy the satisfaction of being able to do something 99.8% of people in this country do not do.

To become a Private Pilot, you must (the following are minimums):

a. Be 17 years old
b. Hold a current Third-Class Medical Certificate
c. Have logged 20 hours minimum of dual instruction with a licensed Flight Instructor
d. Have logged 10 hours minimum of solo flight time, including cross country flights
e. Have logged 40 hours minimum of combined dual instruction and solo time.
f. Pass an FAA written test on aeronautical knowledge.

g. Pass the required practical flight test with an

Recreational and Sport Pilot Certificates

In the past two decades, the FAA has established two additional certificates for recreational and sport pilots. These are intended to allow individuals to learn and enjoy flight, but with limited privileges, such as the number of passengers carried, distances flown, and other limitations. They do allow pilots to enjoy flying, usually limited to a local area, and with restrictions regarding entering controlled airspace, or the size of the aircraft.

FAA authorized examiner.

3. Recreational Pilot Certificate

The Recreational Pilot certificate costs less to get than the Private Pilot certificate and may be way to build flight time and experience in preparation for the Private Pilot certificate. Additional training with an instructor will be required in preparation for the Private Pilot's written and flight tests.

Privileges and Limitations: The Recreational Pilot may fly an airplane with up to four seats but is limited to carrying only one passenger. There are other limitations such as you are limited to cross-country flights of no more than 50 nautical miles from your home airport. This can be extended with additional training and instructor endorsements. A Recreational Pilot may not fly for compensation or hire and may not fly in furtherance of a business.

Requirements: To become a Recreational Pilot, you must (the following are minimums):

a. Be 17 years old
b. Hold a current Third-Class Medical Certificate
c. Have logged 20 Hours minimum of dual instruction with a licensed Flight Instructor
d. Have logged 10 hours minimum of solo flight time
e. Have logged 30 hours minimum of combined dual instruction and solo time.
f. Study for, or take a class for, and pass an FAA written test on aeronautical knowledge.
g. Pass the required practical flight test with an FAA authorized examiner.

4. Sport Pilot Certificate

The Sport Pilot certificate costs even less than the Private Pilot and Recreational Pilot certificates. It is intended to make it possible for individuals to fly in a limited way to enjoy flight. This may also be a way to build flight time and experience in preparation for the Private Pilot certificate. Additional training with an instructor will be required in preparation for the Private Pilot's written and flight tests.

Privileges and Limitations: The Sport Pilot may fly an airplane with no more than two seats and may carry only one passenger. There are other limitations such as you are limited to cross-country flights of no more than 50 nautical miles from your home airport. This can be extended with additional training and instructor endorsements. A Sport Pilot may not fly for compensation or hire and may not fly in furtherance of a business.

The Sport Pilot is also limited to flying an aircraft that has a maximum forward airspeed of 87 knots, unless you have logged dual instruction time in and have an instructor's indorsement to fly an aircraft with a forward airspeed in excess of 87 knots.

Requirements: To become a Sport Pilot, you must (the following are minimums):

a. Be 17 years old
b. Hold a current Third-Class Medical Certificate OR a current, valid US driver's license
c. Have logged 15 Hours minimum of dual instruction with a licensed Flight Instructor
d. Have logged 5 hours minimum of solo flight time
e. Have logged 20 hours minimum of combined dual instruction and solo time.
f. Study for, or take a class for, and pass an FAA written test on aeronautical knowledge.

Pass the required practical flight test with an FAA authorized examiner.

5. Instrument Rating

The instrument rating is included here because it may be added to the Private Pilot Certificate. Once earned, the instrument rating is applicable to other aircraft, including multi-engine and other higher performance aircraft. Additional training and practice may be required for aircraft with advanced navigation systems and for higher performance aircraft.

Privileges: The instrument rated pilot may fly in controlled airspace under less that VFR visibilities. This requires the pilot to file an instrument flight rules (IFR) flight plan and have logged the necessary training, practice, and demonstrated proficiency to fly an instrument-equipped aircraft by reference solely to instruments from immediately after takeoff until just before landing.

Requirements:

    a. Hold at least a current Private Pilot's Certificate
    b. Have logged at least 50 hours of cross-country flight.
    c. Have logged 10 hours of the cross-country flight in airplane equipped for instrument flying
    d. Have logged 40 Hours of actual or simulated instrument flight time
    e. Have logged 15 hours if instrument flight training from an authorized flight instructor
    f. Have flown a cross-country flight of 250 or more nautical miles under IFR rules

g. made an Instrument approach at each airport
h. Three different kinds of instrument approaches
i. Three hours instrument training within two calendar months of the examination date.
i. Pass an FAA written test on aeronautical knowledge.
j. Pass the required practical flight test with an FAA authorized examiner.

Chapter 3. What Will I Learn and Practice to Become a Private Pilot?

1. Academic Training

Whether at your local airport, a university program, or a military program your academic training will include:

a. Aerodynamics - Basically how and why aircraft fly.
b. Federal Aviation Regulations – The rules of the road for pilots
c. Weather – Pilots must understand weather and its importance to flying
d. Aircraft Systems – From engines and engine operation to the operation and use of all flight controls and instrument in the aircraft
e. Navigation – Using navigation charts and navigation instruments in the aircraft
f. Emergency procedures – What to do in the unlikely event if something goes wrong including everything from engine failures to electrical system problems.
g. Radio communications – How to communicate with Air Traffic Control, Control Towers, etc.

2. Flight Training

What Will I Learn and Practice during Flight Training?

a. Basic Preflight activities including flight planning, performing the pre-flight aircraft inspection, engine start, and maneuvering the aircraft on the ground around other aircraft.

b. Preflight engine and systems checks just before takeoff. Most piston aircraft have dual ignitions systems—a safety feature that prevents total engine failure if an ignition system fails. This is a check that is always performed before each flight and includes setting all instruments and radios as required for the flight.

c. Airport communications and how to determine when it is safe to enter the runway in preparation for takeoff, what other aircraft are in the area, etc.

d. Takeoff, climb, and departure.

e. Climb, maintaining airspeed, being vigilant for other aircraft, maintaining heading and navigation by reference to visual landmarks.

f. Basic aircraft maneuvers such as climbs and descents and coordinated turns and maintaining straight and level flight at a set cruise speed, and at slower speeds.

g. More aggressive maneuvers such as steep turns and aerodynamic stalls and stall recovery.

h. Returning to the airport, including radio and traffic pattern procedures.

i. Approach and landing procedures.

j. Post flight procedures.

How long will each flight be? - Initially, training flights will last approximately an hour to an hour-and-a-half. Each flight will allow you to practice what you have learned and usually add additional skills. You will spend 30 to 40 minutes practicing basic and advanced maneuvers and then return to the airport to practice landings.

How Will My Training Progress? - After five to ten hours, your instructor will endorse your logbook for solo flight, and you will fly several supervised solo flights—flights where your instructor is in contact with you via radio.

a. Later, you will learn, and then practice, cross-country flights to different airports, and navigation using charts and aircraft instruments.
b. You will review and study for the written aeronautical knowledge test for the Private Pilot Certificate.
c. Finally, after 35-40 hours, you will practice and review everything for your check ride.

A similar process will be repeated for each additional aeronautical certificate and rating you add.

Chapter 4. Flying for Hire/Professionally

For many pilots, the goal is to be able to earn a living as a pilot. There are many professional aviation opportunities. Most pilots will start off working part-time, either as flight instructors or as air taxi pilots carrying passengers or cargo either on sightseeing flights to on short trips to other airports.

1. Flight Instructor Rating

Of course, someone must teach these other pilots how to fly, so there is a demand for good flight instructors. There are two kinds of flight instructors: (1) those who are using the flight instruction time to build their own flying time (they still must be good instructors) and (2) career instructors that enjoy the challenge of teaching. Being a flight instructor is typically the first paying job for an aspiring professional pilot. It is also a very good way to gain valuable experience and build time.

Requirements:

    a. Hold at least a commercial pilot's certificate or an airline transport pilot certificate
    b. Be at least 18 years old
    c. Have an Instrument rating
    d. Have logged at least 250 hours of flight time
    e. Instructor's logbook endorsement to take knowledge test

f. Pass the required knowledge test
g. Instructor's endorsement of stall awareness, spin entry, spins, and spin recovery.
h. Instructor's logbook endorsement for the practical flight test
i. Pass the required practical flight test
j. Have logged a minimum of 15 hours in the category and class aircraft appropriate to the instructor rating sought.

2. Commercial Pilot Certificate

Air Taxi Pilots fly passengers and/or cargo for hire on demand. Most flights are shorter range flights and the pilots are home for the evening—most of the time. Many Air Taxi pilots have other jobs at the airport such as flight instruction, teaching ground schools, even aircraft maintenance. Some commercial pilots fly for "freight forwarders." This means a major freight/cargo carrier flies into a large hub airport. Cargo is unloaded and sorted by destination, either for local delivery by trucks or loaded on smaller aircraft and forwarded to smaller airports for delivery.

Commercial air taxi pilots typically earn $20,000 to $30,000 per year. But they are building valuable time and experience to qualify for a better position with a regional airline, a professional corporate pilot position, or a major airline.

Requirements:

a. Hold at least a second class medical certificate.

b. Be at least 18 years old
c. Have an instrument rating
d. Have logged 250 hours of flight time
e. Have logged 100 hours in powered aircraft (glider time would count towards total time)
f. Have logged 100 hours of pilot-in-command time
g. Pass the commercial pilot knowledge exam.
h. Have an instructor's logbook endorsement for the practical flight test
i. Pass the required practical flight test

Jobs for Commercial Pilots:

Corporate Business Travel - Top corporate pilots get to fly great, fast equipment, travel to different places, live on an expense account, etc. It is an "on demand" job; flights may leave at odd hours and on short notice.

Mid-to-large businesses often have their own aircraft and pilots. Assume the owner wants to take several key personnel to visit an important client. They can use a corporate aircraft—anything from a smaller twin engine airplane to a corporate style jet—depending on the budget, distance, and importance of the trip.

The travelers set the schedule and destination. Corporate aircraft usually can land at smaller airports closer to their clients. Corporate flying can be much less expensive than using airlines. By setting the schedule and flying directly to closer airports, passengers arrive refreshed, can complete their business, and be home for dinner. Being a corporate pilot usually means flying good equipment, but it also means you must be ready to go wherever and whenever the boss wants to travel.

To be a corporate pilot means you must have a commercial pilot certificate with an instrument rating, and it also means you have several hundred hours of flying experience just to fly as a copilot. Many corporate pilots who fly the latest business jet aircraft will have Airline Transport Pilot certificates.

Aerial application - Better known as "crop dusting," aerial application is a specialized field, but for pilots who enjoy the challenge of flying an airplane to its limits and accomplishing something useful, this could be the ticket. It requires precise flying, total concentration, landing on dirt roads, and working as quickly as possible. Most crop dusting, or "aerial application" airplanes are single-seat aircraft. Training is basically done "on the job" by an experienced crop duster pilot. Work is either seasonal or operators move around the country to meet regional requirements.

Aerial Photography / Survey - These are specialized flying jobs that pilots are contracted for. Many of these aircraft are equipped with survey or photographic equipment and may require an operator in addition to the pilot. Typically, the pilots have other roles in the companies for which they work.

Test Pilot / Aircraft Demonstration Pilot - Most aircraft manufacturers have test and demonstration pilots on staff. These are usually additional duties for engineers, mechanics, even sales people. Demonstration pilots take prospective buyers or demonstration flights. Most manufacturers, including even kit manufacturers for experimental aircraft, have pilots on staff to take aircraft to major airshows and events around the country, even around the world.

3. Airline Transport Pilot Certificate

Being an airline pilot has its demands and its benefits. First officers can earn up to $100,000 a year while Captains may earn $200,000. Both will travel with all expenses covered and company benefits of free or low-cost travel when off duty on their own airline and often with other airlines. It is a demanding job, being away from home for several days to a week or more at a time. For example, new rules limit pilots to a maximum of 60 hours of flight duty per week, defined as 168 consecutive hours of duty time. In any consecutive 28-day period, a pilot cannot exceed 290 hours of duty time, of which no more than 100 can be flight time. During 365 consecutive days, pilots cannot exceed 1,000 hours flight time. "Duty Time" is all time that the pilot is "on the clock" and includes pre-flight, post-flight activities, and layover time.

An ATP is required for any scheduled airline operation. So most younger ATP holders fly for commuter and regional airlines early in their careers to build time and experience.

Below, the flight time requirement of 1,500 hours is the maximum requirement. Former military pilots need only 750 hours total time. Graduates from a Part 141 program in at approved four-year universities with a bachelor's degree need have only 1,000 hours, including 200 hours of cross-country time. Pilots that have accumulated at least 30 credit hours, or who have completed an approved Associate's degree program can apply for the ATP check ride with 1,250 hours total time and 200 hours of cross-country time.

Pilots, as of 2014, must complete the Airline Transport Pilot Certification Training Program (ATP CTP) before completing the FAA written exam. This is a combined classroom and flight simulator training course. All airlines, both regional and major airline pilot applicants are expected to take this training before taking the ATP written exam. Many colleges with flight training programs may also offer ATP CTP training.

Requirements

a. Hold at least a commercial pilot's certificate with an instrument rating
b. Be at least 21 years old
c. Have logged 1,500 hours of flight time (there are exceptions)
d. Have logged 200 hours logged cross-country time
e. Have logged 100 hours of night flight time
f. Have logged 50 hours of multi-engine time.
g. Have logged 75 hours of instrument time (25 hours can be in a flight simulator)
h. Have logged 250 hours of pilot in command (PIC) time.

i. Completed the ATP CTP Training as applicable
j. Pass the required practical flight test

Chapter 5. Other Types of Flying

1. Helicopter Pilot

Helicopters are rotorcraft which simply means that instead of wings, the aircraft uses rotors to generate lift and forward motion. This group also includes autogyros that are aircraft with both a conventional aircraft engine and propeller and rotors that turn as the aircraft moves through the air. Autogyros are primarily sport aircraft.

Helicopter careers range from tour flights, and offshore oil and gas support to law enforcement, emergency medical services, and commuter and intercity transportation. Helicopters are also used in agricultural aerial applications and search and rescue, as well as in helicopter flight instruction.

The training and experience requirements for helicopter pilots are similar to those of fixed wing pilots and include private and commercial pilot certificates and instrument ratings.

Requirements

To become a Private Pilot, you must (the following are minimums):

a. Be 17 years old
b. Hold a current Third-Class Medical Certificate
c. Have logged 20 hours minimum of dual instruction with a licensed Flight Instructor

d. Have logged 10 hours minimum of solo flight time, including cross country flights
e. Have logged 40 hours minimum of combined dual instruction and solo time.
f. Pass an FAA written test on aeronautical knowledge.
g. Pass the required practical flight test with an FAA authorized examiner.

To apply for a Commercial helicopter certificate, the pilot must have a total of 150 hours flight time with at least 50 hours of helicopter time. The least expensive way to obtain the Commercial Helicopter license is to first get a fixed wind private pilot certificate and build experience flying. Once you have accumulated 100 hours, transition to helicopter training and build flight time to 50 hours in helicopters.

2. Glider Private Pilot

Glider or sailplane flying is essentially a sport or recreational activity. Commercial glider pilots are primarily employed to provide flights for paying customers and if instructor qualified, provide instruction to aspiring glider pilots.

Under the right conditions, gliders can be flown for long distances and remain aloft for hours. A typical sightseeing flight lasts approximately 20 to 30 minutes. Training flights may last only 10 minutes. Gliders must be launched, usually by a tow plane that pulls the glider aloft and, once at the desired altitude, the tow line is released, and gliding flight begins.

Requirements

After solo, student pilots may qualify as a Private Pilot-Glider provided they:

a. Be 16 years of age; and
b. Logged at least 10 hours of flight time in a glider
c. Logged at least 20 total glider flights
d. Have 2 hours of solo flight time in a glider
e. Pass the FAA written examination
f. Pass the flight exam with a FAA Examiner.

3. Lighter-than-Air (Hot Air Balloons)

Hot Air Balloons are flown primarily for recreational purposes—except for those pilots who carry passengers for hire.

Requirements

To become a Private Hot Air Balloon pilot, you must:

a. Be 16 years of age
b. Have at least 10 hours including flights with an instructor and solo flights
c. Pass the written FAA knowledge test
d. Pass the practical knowledge test with a flight examiner.

The Commercial Hot Air Balloon Pilot certificate is required to carry passengers for hire and requires

nore training and experience, passing the
Commercial Pilot knowledge test, and a practical
knowledge test with a flight examiner.

Note: Lighter-than-Air aircraft also include blimps.
This is a very specialized niche in aviation, although
there are indications that larger blimps may
eventually be developed and flown for special cargo
and transport missions. Most blimp flight training is
performed on-the-job with blimp operators.
Applicants should already have a commercial pilot's
certificate with an instrument rating.

Chapter 6. Getting Started

First Steps

Embarking on a career in aviation, or even just deciding to become a private pilot requires a commitment of time and money to succeed. Many people have set out to become pilots and run out of money and/or desire before becoming even a private pilot. Planning and perseverance are necessary to succeed. Here are some things you can do to help make both a decision and a personal commitment to becoming a pilot.

Read - It really does not matter what you read—just read books, magazines, etc. about flying and airplanes. Look on line for blogs and articles about flying—read everything from technical articles about airplanes to personal experiences of pilots and their adventures. If you end up saying, "Yes, that's for me," then continue.

Subscribe to one or two aviation magazines and go through them every month.

Go to Local Airports, Talk to Pilots - If you are going to fly, you must go to the airport! Many smaller airports have places where you can simply sit and watch the action and listen to the sounds. People at airports like to talk about flying and show you around the airplanes—it is usually a fun experience.

Listen and ask questions. Every pilot has a story to tell, and since he is there to tell the story, it does not matter how scary it may sound—it was a good experience. (But do not believe every story!)

Understand Medical and Physical Requirements for Different Types of Pilots -

This is where reality begins to set in. Pilots need to be physically able to fly an airplane. At the entry level, as a sport or private pilot, the physical and medical requirements are not demanding. More than 98% of people can pass basic physical requirements.

As your flying responsibilities increase, for example carrying passengers for hire, the medical requirement becomes more detailed. Still, an average healthy person can be expected to pass the physical exam.

Also, there are many examples of amputees and others who might be called handicapped that are still able to pilot an airplane.

Look at Online Videos of Aircraft or Visit Museums -

In this age of "video-everything" there are thousands of videos, most running 15 minutes or less, about almost every kind of aircraft, and every type of flying in every situation.

There are aviation museums in almost every state, often many different museums. Some may be dedicated to a specific make of aircraft, or a military service, or a local celebrity who also had one or more airplanes.

Go to the Nearest Airport -

If you have several airports within a reasonable distance, visit them all.

Talk to the person behind the desk about the types of airplanes they use for training: local airport flight schools may not have advanced aircraft to pursue advanced ratings like multi-engine aircraft. Ask about the costs, scheduling, and training materials. Ask about ground schools versus self-study.

Talk to a flight instructor. He or she will show you around an airplane and explain the process. Talk to other students. If they offer a demonstration flight for a reasonable fee—take it.

The Next Step

You have made up your mind—you want to learn to fly and get your first pilot's license. It is time to determine how you want to get your training.

There are two basic training programs: FAR Part 61 and FAR Part 141.

Part 61 Training at Your Local Airport - This is the way that most pilots start. Any certified instructor pilot can give training under Part 61 of the FARs, and this is the type of training offered at most local airports. In this training, the student accumulates a minimum of 40 hours of dual and solo time before being eligible to take the private pilot check ride. You will also work with your instructor's guidance on studying for the written exam. The instructor may have sessions of one-on-one ground school, or simply give you assignments—whichever way he feels you will learn best. All records of flight and ground training, nd progress will be maintained in your logbook. You will probably pay as you go. You may get a discount if you pay for a block of airplane time—usually 10 hours—in advance.

Part 141 Training - Some flight academies, colleges, and universities are authorized under Part 141. This means they have an FAA-approved curriculum of ground school and structured flight training requirements. It is most common in larger flight training and academic flight training programs. Because of the formal curriculum and structured program, a student may earn his Private Pilot Certificate in just 35 hours in a Part 141 program, and times are also reduced for the Commercial Pilot Certificate. Usually, payment terms will be determined in advance and you will make a commitment to adhere to the program. This is usually the quickest way to get to your first certificate.

Flight Academy Programs - If your goal is to become a working pilot, you may want to consider an academy program. A Part 141 flight academy is a much more structured program than a Part 61 program, usually with formal ground school classes, and regular flying schedules.

1. You will progress more rapidly in an academy environment.
2. Academy training tends to be more professional than Part 61 training.
3. Academies will allow you to progress to advanced certifications if that is your goal.
4. Some academies are associated with an airline, suggesting that their graduates may have an advantage of landing a job with that airline. Keep

in mind that much must be accomplished between getting that first license and qualifying for a prestigious airline position.

A University Aviation Program - There are many Part 141 flight programs available—they may be dedicated to flight and aeronautical training like Embry-Riddle Aeronautical University, or they may be part of a larger college such as Perdue University. Graduates from these programs will earn either a Bachelor's or Associate's Degree in Aviation. The purpose of university programs is for you to graduate as an employable pilot. You should graduate with a Commercial Pilot Certificate with an Instrument Rating. Also, being associated with a college or university program, you will have access to scholarship opportunities and student loans.

Chapter 7. Access to Aircraft

You do not have to own an airplane to enjoy flying regularly. Your local airport will rent you an airplane for an hour, a day, or even for a trip. If you fly only several hours each month, renting costs less than owning.

1. Renting

Many pilots rely on renting aircraft from their local airport, perhaps where they trained. This is the easiest way to have access to an airplane, and it also has the advantage of offering multiple sizes and types of aircraft. If you just want to fly by yourself, you can rent a smaller two-seat airplane at the minimum rate. If you want to take several friends flying, then rent a four-seat airplane. You may even have choices between different makes and styles of aircraft such as a high-wing Cessna or a low-wing Piper or Beechcraft. All you pay is the hourly rental rate that includes all aircraft expenses and fuel.

2. An Aero Club

Many pilots belong to an aero club. This is usually a group of pilots who have joined forces to buy one or two aircraft and share the expenses. Members can schedule airplanes when they are available and are usually able to fly when they want to. Members pay an initial membership fee, monthly dues, and a lesser hourly fee (compared to just renting) for flying. If you plan to fly more than 10 hours a month, say building time for advanced ratings, you may save money over renting. Aero clubs usually have slightly newer, better equipped aircraft. Larger clubs will have several different types of aircraft to choose from.

3. Owner

Owning your own aircraft always seems like "the thing to do." This, however, is usually the most expensive way to have access to an aircraft. The advantage is that you have total access and can fly when you want. Once you own the aircraft, your expenses are fuel and oil, maintenance, hangar or parking space at the airport, and insurance. Maintenance includes required annual inspections that cost $200-$300 or more, depending on the type of aircraft, and much more if any work is required.

4. Leaseback

Owners sometimes put their personal aircraft on "leaseback" with an aero club or the local flight school at the airport. The flight school will use your aircraft as part of their fleet, charge pilots for your aircraft just as they do for any rental, and pay you an hourly rate for the aircraft's use. They pay for fuel and may include your airplane on their insurance. You are still responsible for any maintenance and inspections on the aircraft. And, of course, if you go to the airport to fly, it may be out on a flight.

5. Partnership

You and one or several other pilots may enter into a legal partnership to own and maintain an aircraft together. The more owners, the less each must pay, but also the more pilots that will be flying and sharing the aircraft. Most partnerships allow pilots access to newer or higher performance aircraft.

6. Experimental Aircraft

One way to have your own aircraft is to build one yourself. Homebuilt or kit-built aircraft are very popular for anyone who wants to own a new aircraft for the cost well below that of a production aircraft.

Builders may build from scratch, that is using plans and raw materials and parts to build a plane. Many builders prefer kits that include many preformed and preassembled parts. This speeds up the building process for most pilots.

One advantage of the homebuilt aircraft is that you can install any engine you want and equip the aircraft with the instruments you need for your flying. Some home-built aircraft are just a basic aircraft while other can be equipped for full instruments, powerful engines, even pressurized for flying at high altitudes for long distances.

Most kit planes take several years to complete. All kit-built or home-built aircraft are registered as "Experimental" aircraft and may not be used for hire.

Many kit manufacturers offer factory-assist programs. You buy the kit and it is delivered to the kit manufacturer's facilities. You go to the that facility and, with the aid of airframe and engine mechanics, build your airplane. Most such programs make it possible to have your aircraft assembled and airworthy in as little as six months. Of course, there is an additional fee for these programs.

Chapter 8. Military Aviation

1. Become a Military Pilot

One of the best ways, but certainly not the easiest, to get into flying is to be accepted into one of the military flight training programs. You will be able to fly some of the best equipment available, receive exceptional training, and be earning a salary from the day you enlist.

Each branch of the military has a specific mission, and the flying in each service supports that mission. The Air Force is the dedicated air arm of the military performing both major supply and combat roles. While the Air Force's fighters attract most of the attention, most Air Force pilots are busy delivering personnel, supplies, and munitions to bases around the world. Many pilots fly military versions of commercial airliners and other transport equipment that is very similar.

If an occasional supersonic dash is what you want, both the Air Force and the Navy can satisfy the "need for speed." But only the Navy can provide the thrill of catapult shot takeoffs and arresting hook landings.

If defying gravity by hovering in one spot, taking off and landing vertically, or flying with a heavy truck suspended beneath your aircraft, look to the Army's helicopter program.

There are three routes into the military that offer access to flight training. The surest, but most challenging route is to be accepted to one of the pension, at age 42, probably at the rank of Major. This pilot would be in an excellent position to transition to a major airline with a second career in aviation.

3. Types of Military Flying

As you prepare to graduate from flight training, the military may offer you the chance to indicate your preferences for assignment. The first rule of assignments, however, is that "the needs of the service" will be the final determination of your assignment.

Fighter Aircraft: There are pros and cons to each assignment. For example, fighter pilots will get to fly some of the highest performance aircraft available. Most flights, however, are relatively short duration flights, less than two hours, except for occasional long-duration, long-distance flights. Fighter pilots do not build flight time as quickly as transport pilots. Career pilots, however, will have plenty of time to build valuable experience, whatever they fly.

Transport Aircraft: Pilots flying transport aircraft will be part of a crew and will log more time per flight. If your objective is to leave the service at the earliest possible date and seek and airline job, flying transport aircraft is the best way to build time and relevant experience.

4. An Alternate Career in Aviation—The Army

If you want first class aviation training and do not have a college degree, the Army allows you to go from High School to Flight School—for helicopters.

The program allows high school graduates to apply and train to become warrant officers, the rank necessary to attend Army Aviation School.

The application process requires you to write an essay, get letters of recommendation, and meet the same medical and physical requirements as every other Army flight school candidate.

A Career as an Army Helicopter Pilot: Once you have mastered flight school, you will be assigned to any one of more than two dozen Aviation Regiments in the Army, Army Reserves, or Air National Guard. The best of the best Army pilots and crew members tryout for the Army's Special Operations Aviation Regiment.

Current Army aircraft include:

a. TH-67 (Bell 206B) Trainer
b. OH-58 Kiowa Warrior, Trainer and Light Attack
c. AH-64 Attack Helicopters
d. UH-60 Blackhawk Multi-role
e. CH-47 twin-rotor Chinook Transport
f. UH-72 Lakota Utility/Medivac
g. MH-6 Little Bird Special Ops Support

h. C-12 Huron fixed-wing personnel transport

Chapter 8. Health and Flying

Personal health is important for pilots.

Pilots are required to obtain an Airman Medical Certificate from and Airman Medical Examiner for all pilot ratings except the Sport Pilot Certificate. The different levels of medical certificate requirements are associated with the level of pilot certification and responsibility.

Third Class Medical: Private pilots must hold a Third Class medical certificate. Under current rules, for pilots under the age of 40, the Third Class medical certificate is valid for 60 calendar months. For pilots 50 years and older, the certificate is valid for 24 calendar months.

Second Class Medical: To exercise the privileges of a Commercial pilot, the pilot must hold a Second Class medical certificate, and the certificate is valid for 12 calendar months regardless of the pilot's age.

First Class Medical: Under current rules, airline transport pilots must hold a First Class medical certificate. For ATP pilots under the age of 40, the First Class medical certificate is valid for 12 calendar months. For pilots 50 years and older, the certificate is valid for 6 calendar months.

Note: The FAA has recently made changes in medical requirements. The above data is current as of this printing but are subject to change. Aviation medical examiners must follow the "Summary of Medical Standards."

Printed in the USA
CPSIA information can be obtained
at www.ICGtesting.com
LVHW021402261023
762067LV00004B/11

9 781950 864492